jack johnson.
on and on

Transcribed by Jeff Jacobson and Steve Gorenberg

Album art direction and design by Dave Lively/Courtesy of Universal Records
Cover photo by Scott Soens
Interior photography by Danny Clinch

ISBN 1-57560-691-7

Copyright © 2004 Cherry Lane Music Company
International Copyright Secured   All Rights Reserved

The music, text, design and graphics in this publication are protected by copyright law. Any duplication or transmission,
by any means, electronic, mechanical, photocopying, recording or otherwise, is an infringement of copyright.

Visit our website at www.cherrylane.com

We recorded "On and on" in Hawaii during August 2002. My brother Trent and I built the studio with a little help from our friends. Trent did most of the work (he calls me the sissy musician).

We spent about three weeks recording and one week mixing. We played a lot of ping pong and sometimes it was difficult getting everyone into the studio when the waves were good or the weather was nice, but eventually we finished.

Adam, Merlo, and I wanted the record to have a laid back feel to it. Mario and Robert seemed to understand what we were going for and the whole experience was smooth.

I feel very fortunate to get to share my music with people and I'm flattered that someone would want to learn how to play my songs. I learned guitar chords from a friend named Peff, and after that I would bug my mom to buy me music books (mostly Hendrix and Marley). It blows my mind that this book is full of my songs. I hope you enjoy.

Aloha, Jack

LILLO'S SCHOOL OF MODERN MUSIC LTD.
10848 Whyte Avenue
EDMONTON, ALBERTA T6E 2B3
(780) 433-0138

contents

TIMES LIKE THESE

Words and Music by
Jack Johnson

Copyright © 2003 by Bubble Toes Publishing (ASCAP)
All Rights Administered by Universal Music Corp.
All Rights Reserved   Used by Permission

6

THE HORIZON HAS BEEN DEFEATED

Words and Music by
Jack Johnson

*Chord symbols reflect overall harmony.

Copyright © 2003 by Bubble Toes Publishing (ASCAP)
All Rights Administered by Universal Music Corp.
All Rights Reserved   Used by Permission

TRAFFIC IN THE SKY

Words and Music by
Jack Johnson

Copyright © 2003 by Bubble Toes Publishing (ASCAP)
All Rights Administered by Universal Music Corp.
All Rights Reserved   Used by Permission

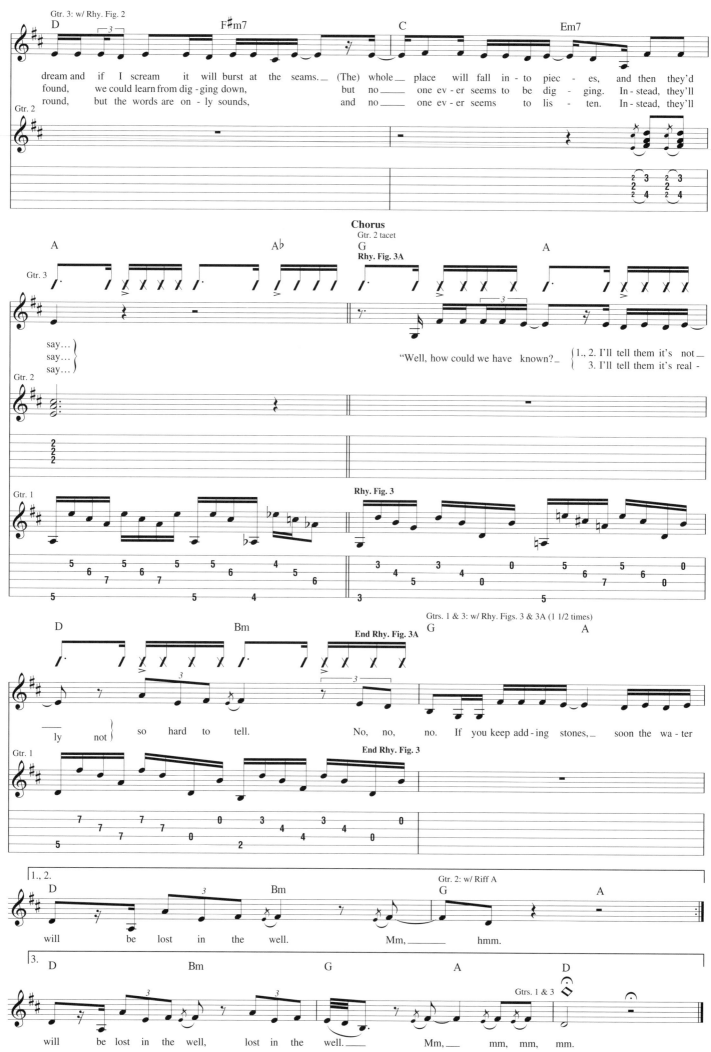

TAYLOR

Words and Music by
Jack Johnson

*Chord symbols reflect implied harmony.

1. They say

Copyright © 2003 by Bubble Toes Publishing (ASCAP)
All Rights Administered by Universal Music Corp.
All Rights Reserved   Used by Permission

14

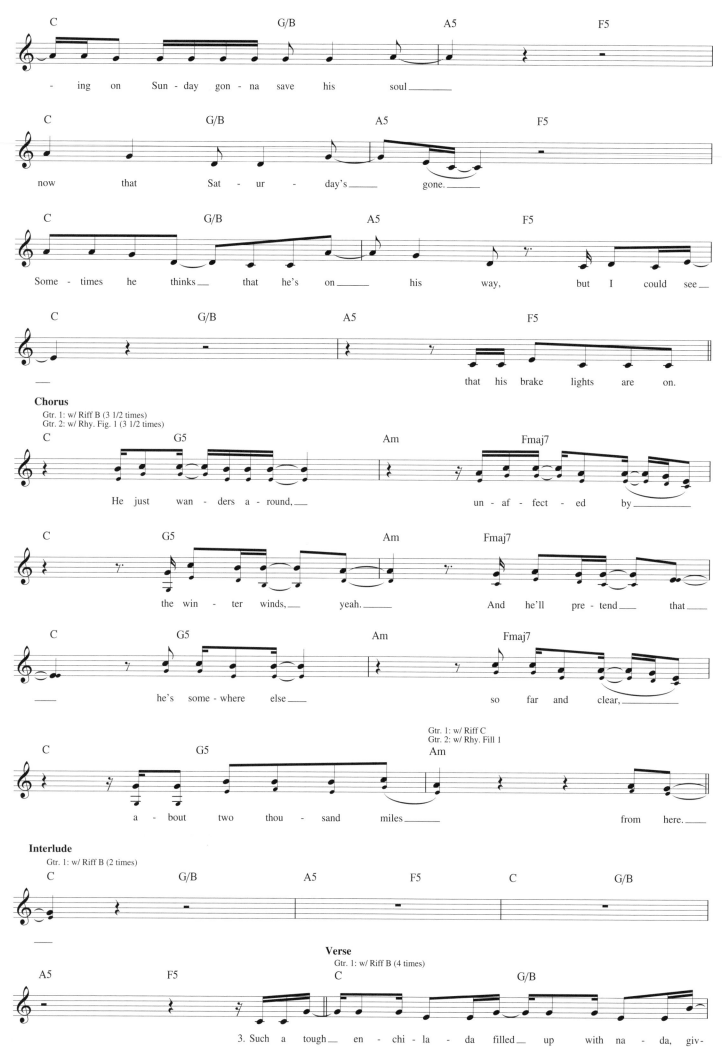

Chorus
Gtr. 1: w/ Riff B (3 1/2 times)
Gtr. 2: w/ Rhy. Fig. 1 (3 1/2 times)

Gtr. 1: w/ Riff C
Gtr. 2: w/ Rhy. Fill 1

Interlude
Gtr. 1: w/ Riff B (2 times)

Verse
Gtr. 1: w/ Riff B (4 times)

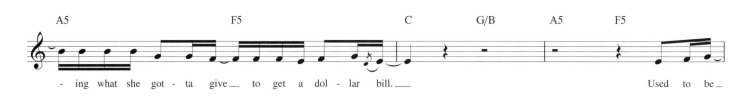

-ing what she got-ta give__ to get a dol-lar bill.__ Used to be__

__ a lim-ber chick-en, times__ a been a tick-ing; now__ she's fin-ger lick-ing to the man__ with the

mon-ey in his pock-et, fly-ing in his rock-et, on-__ly stop-ping by on his way to a bet-ter world.__

Bridge

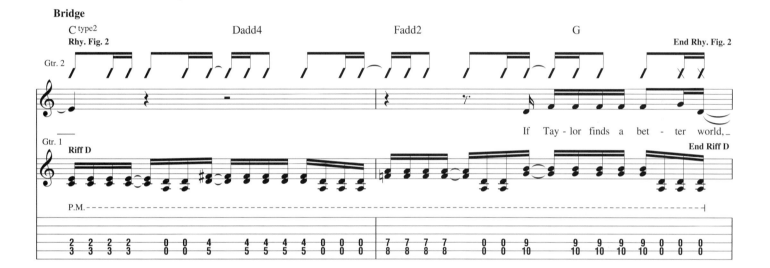

If Tay-lor finds a bet-ter world,__

Outro

Gtr. 1: w/ Riff D
Gtr. 2: w/ Rhy. Fig. 2

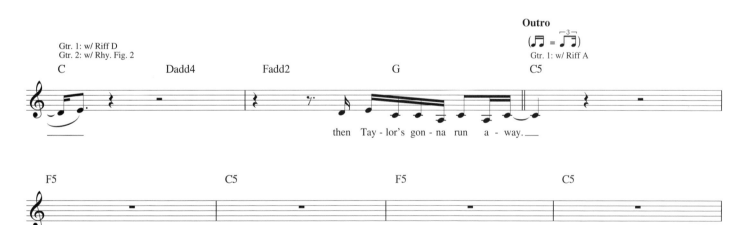

then Tay-lor's gon-na run a-way.__

A little slower

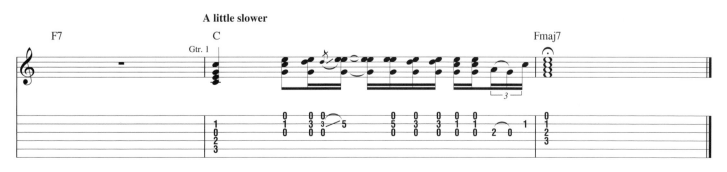

GONE

Words and Music by
Jack Johnson

Intro

Moderately slow ♩ = 100

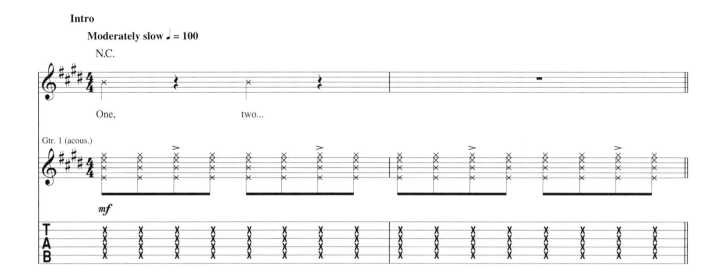

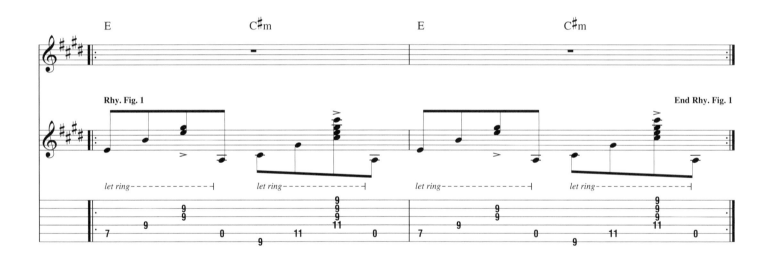

Verse

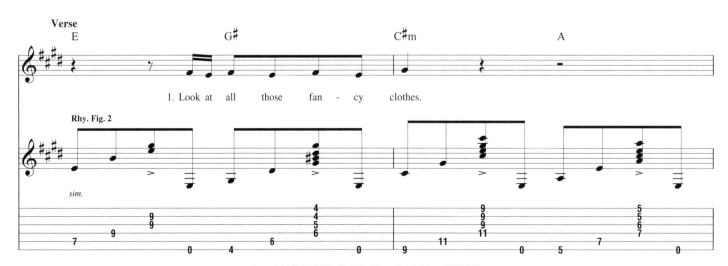

1. Look at all those fan - cy clothes.

Copyright © 2003 by Bubble Toes Publishing (ASCAP)
All Rights Administered by Universal Music Corp.
All Rights Reserved   Used by Permission

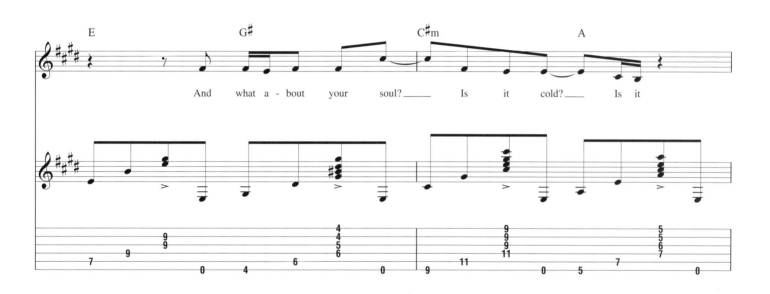

CUPID

Words and Music by
Jack Johnson

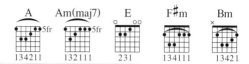

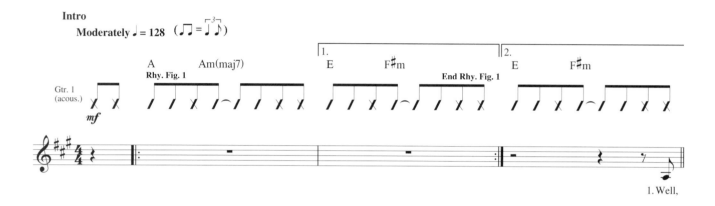

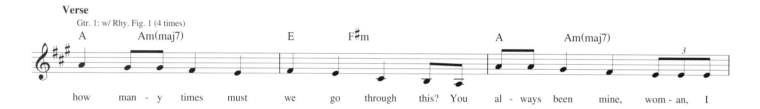

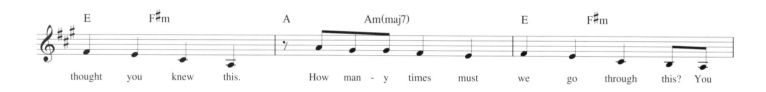

Copyright © 2003 by Bubble Toes Publishing (ASCAP)
All Rights Administered by Universal Music Corp.
All Rights Reserved   Used by Permission

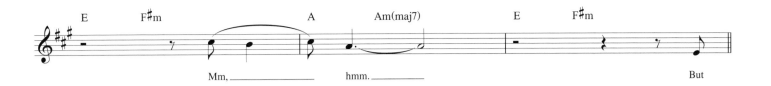

E   F#m   A   Am(maj7)   E   F#m

Mm, _____ hmm. _____   But

Chorus

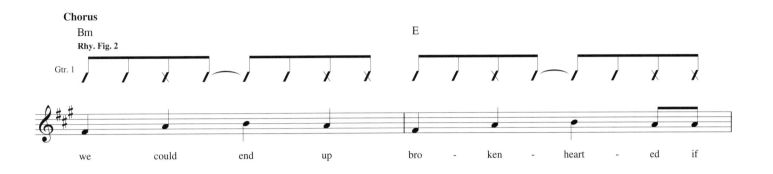

Bm   E

Rhy. Fig. 2

Gtr. 1

we   could   end   up   bro - ken - heart - ed if

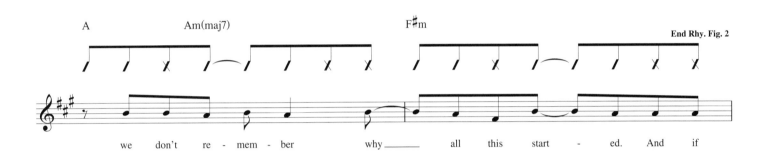

A   Am(maj7)   F#m   **End Rhy. Fig. 2**

we   don't   re - mem - ber   why _____ all   this   start - ed. And   if

Gtr. 1: w/ Rhy. Fig. 2 (1 1/2 times)

Bm   E   A   Am(maj7)

they   try   to   tell   you   love   fades   with   time, _____ tell   them   there's   no   such   thing   as

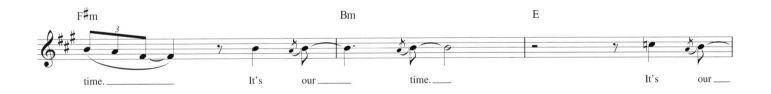

F#m   Bm   E

time. _____   It's   our _____ time. _____   It's   our _____

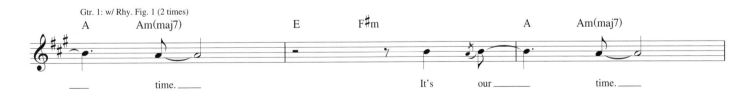

Gtr. 1: w/ Rhy. Fig. 1 (2 times)

A   Am(maj7)   E   F#m   A   Am(maj7)

_____ time. _____   It's   our _____ time. _____

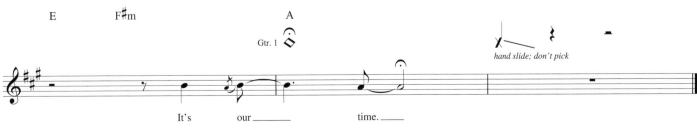

E   F#m   A

Gtr. 1

hand slide; don't pick

It's   our _____ time. _____

WASTING TIME

Words and Music by Jack Johnson,
Merlo Podlewski and Adam Topol

Copyright © 2003 by Bubble Toes Publishing (ASCAP), TRPKL Music Publishing (BMI) and Adam Topol Music (BMI)
All Rights for Bubble Toes Publishing Administered by Universal Music Corp.
All Rights Reserved   Used by Permission

24

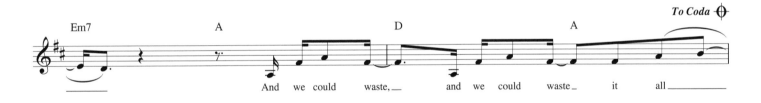

Interlude

Coda

Chorus

Yeah,___ but ev - 'ry - bod - y thinks that ev - 'ry - bod - y knows a - bout ev-

- 'ry - bod - y else, no, no, no - bod - y knows an - y - thing a - bout___ them - selves___ 'cause they're

___ all wor - ried a - bout ev - 'ry - bod - y else, yeah.   Oh. _____

Outro

And we could waste... _   Do, do, do, do, do, do, do.

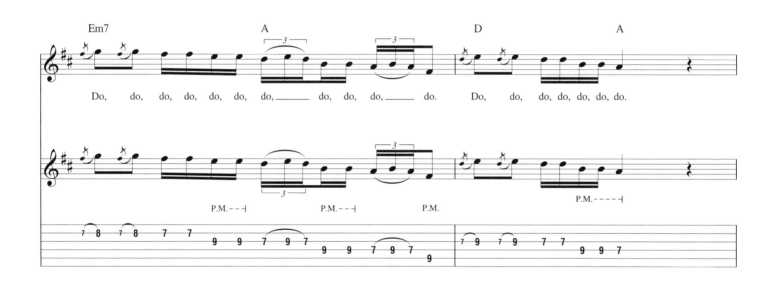

Do, do, do, do, do, do, do, ___ do, do, do, ___ do.   Do, do, do, do, do, do, do.

Do, do, do, do, do, do, do, ___ do, do, do, ___ do, do, do.

*Gtr. 1 to left of slash in tab.

28

HOLES TO HEAVEN

Words and Music by
Jack Johnson

Copyright © 2003 by Bubble Toes Publishing (ASCAP)
All Rights Administered by Universal Music Corp.
All Rights Reserved   Used by Permission

29

There we were _ stuck in _ } Port Blaire, _ where boats break _ and chil - dren stare. _
mov - ing back _ north to _ }

Chorus
2nd time, Gtr. 4: w/ Riff C

There were so _ man - y few - er ques - tions when _ stars were still just the holes _ to heav -

Riff C
Gtr. 4 (elec.)

mf
w/ clean tone

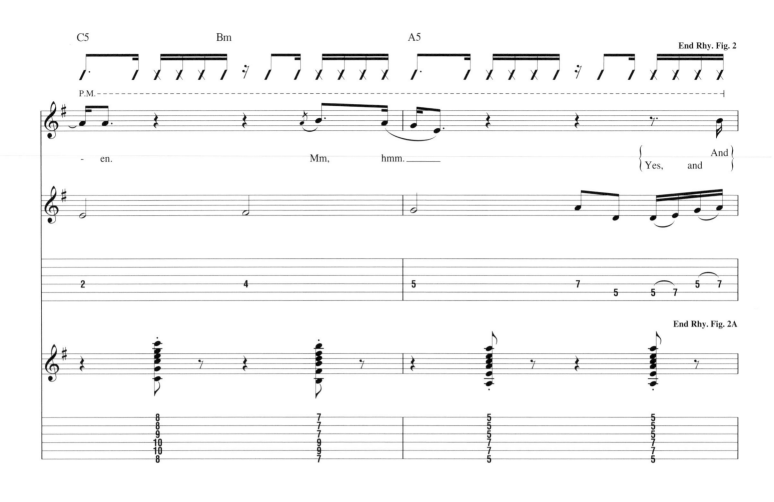

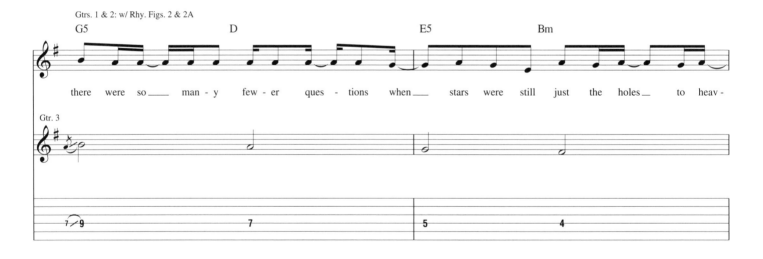

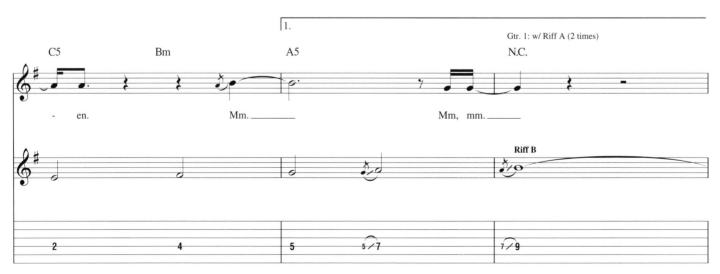

DREAMS BE DREAMS

Words and Music by
Jack Johnson

*Chord symbols reflect overall harmony.

**Lightly hit strings w/ R.H.

Verse

Gtr. 1: w/ Riff B (4 times)

1. She's ___ just wait - ing for the sum - mer - time, ___ when the weath - er's fine. ___

Copyright © 2003 by Bubble Toes Publishing (ASCAP)
All Rights Administered by Universal Music Corp.
All Rights Reserved   Used by Permission

She could hitch a ride__ out of __ town and so far a - way__ from that low - down,__

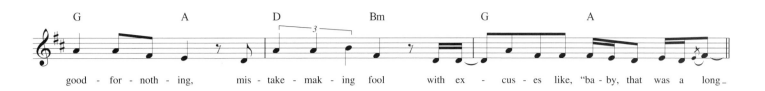

good - for - noth - ing, mis - take - mak - ing fool with ex - cus - es like, "ba - by, that was a long__

Chorus

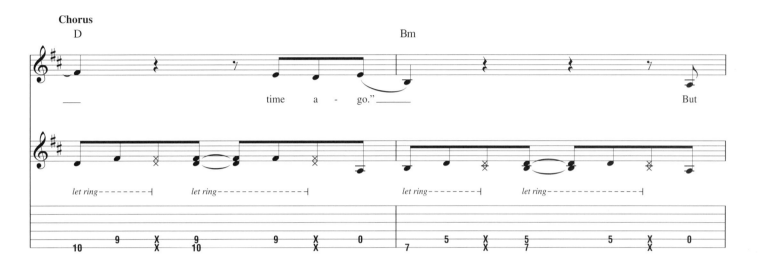

__ time a - go." __ But

let ring *let ring* *let ring* *let ring*

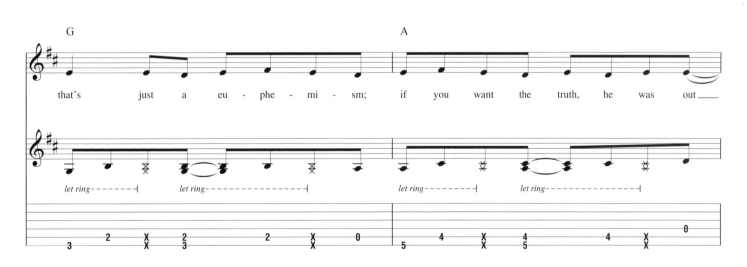

that's just a eu - phe - mi - sm; if you want the truth, he was out __

let ring *let ring* *let ring* *let ring*

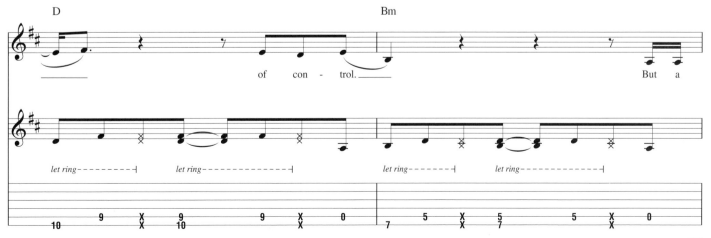

__ of con - trol. __ But a

let ring *let ring* *let ring* *let ring*

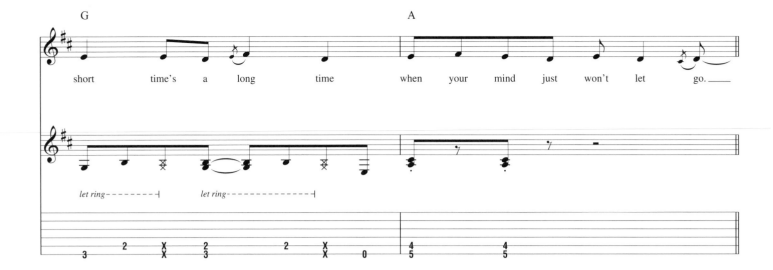

short time's a long time when your mind just won't let go.

Interlude

Gtr. 1: w/ Riff A

Guitar Solo

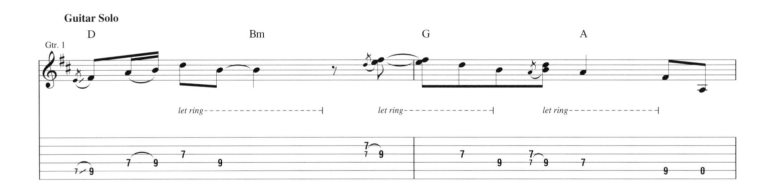

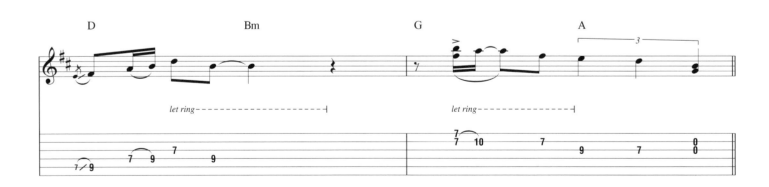

Verse

Gtr. 1: w/ Riff B (6 times)

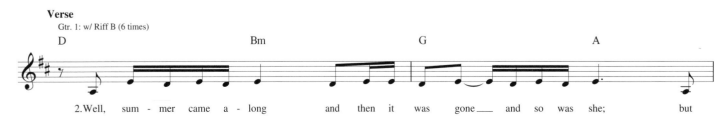

2. Well, sum - mer came a - long and then it was gone ___ and so was she; but

not from him, ____ 'cause he fol - lowed her ____ just to let her know ____ her

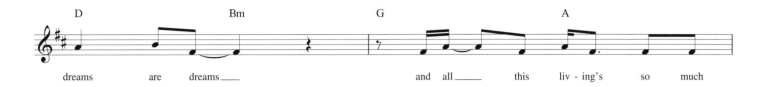

dreams are dreams ____ and all ____ this liv - ing's so much

hard - er than it seems. ____ But, girl, ____ don't ____ let your

dreams be dreams. ____ You know ____ this liv - ing's not so

hard as it seems. ____ Don't ____ let ____ your

Outro

Gtr. 1: w/ Riff B (1 1/2 times)

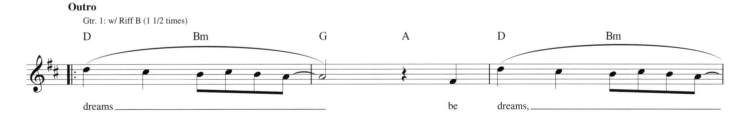

dreams _____ be dreams, _____

____ your ____ be dreams.

TOMORROW MORNING

Words and Music by
Jack Johnson

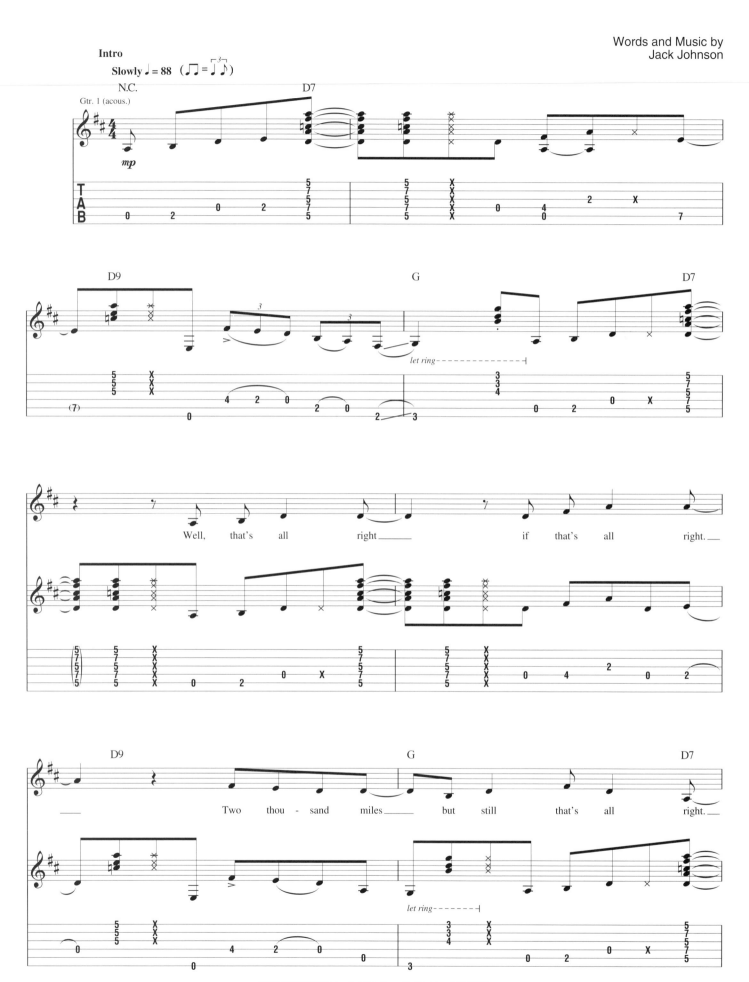

Copyright © 2003 by Bubble Toes Publishing (ASCAP)
All Rights Administered by Universal Music Corp.
All Rights Reserved   Used by Permission

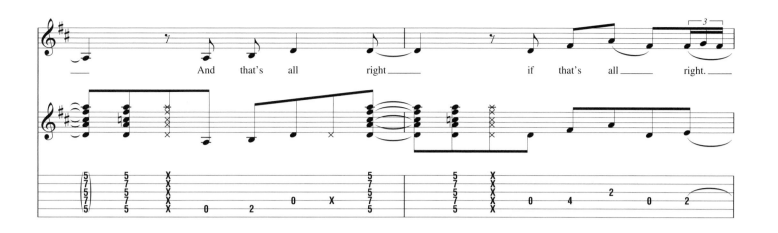

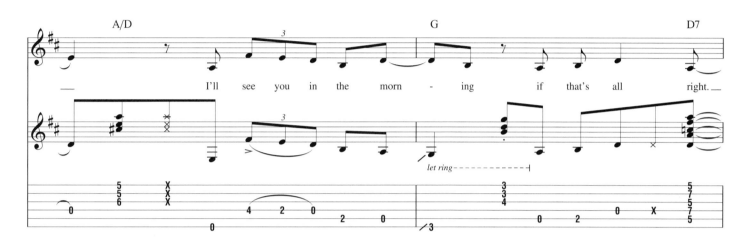

Slower ♩ = 72 (♫ = ♩♪)

Verse

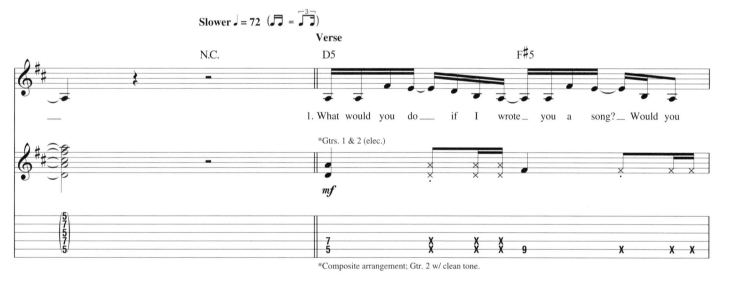

*Composite arrangement; Gtr. 2 w/ clean tone.

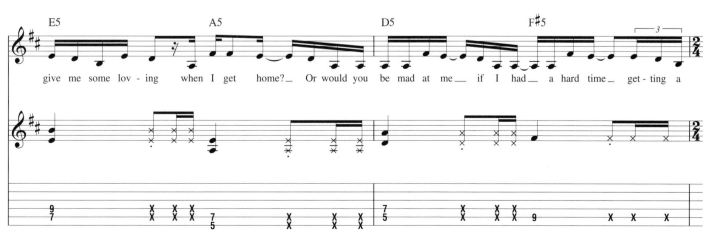

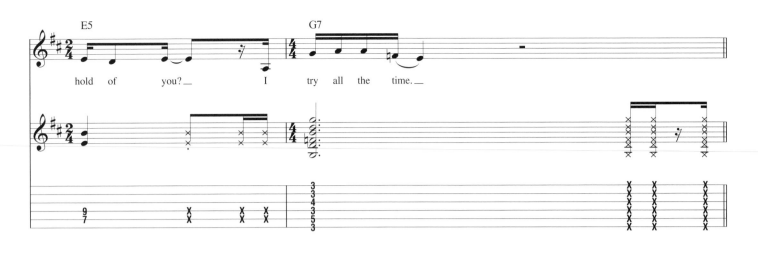

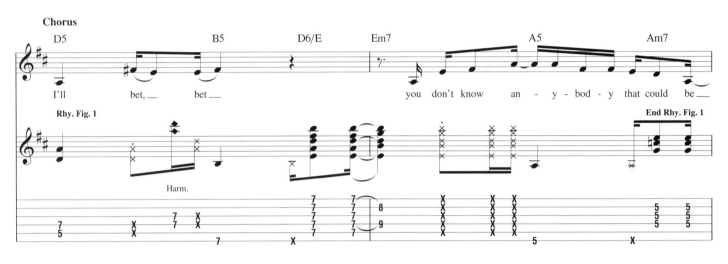

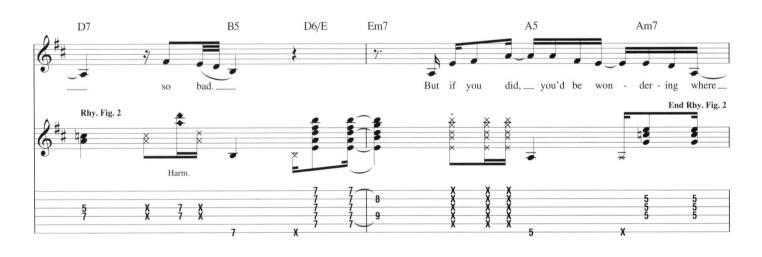

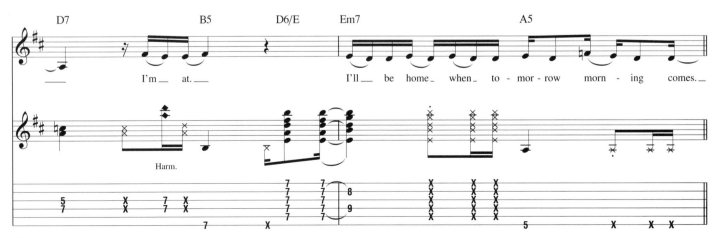

FALL LINE

Words and Music by
Jack Johnson

Copyright © 2003 by Bubble Toes Publishing (ASCAP)
All Rights Administered by Universal Music Corp.
All Rights Reserved   Used by Permission

COOKIE JAR

Words and Music by
Jack Johnson

Copyright © 2003 by Bubble Toes Publishing (ASCAP)
All Rights Administered by Universal Music Corp.
All Rights Reserved   Used by Permission

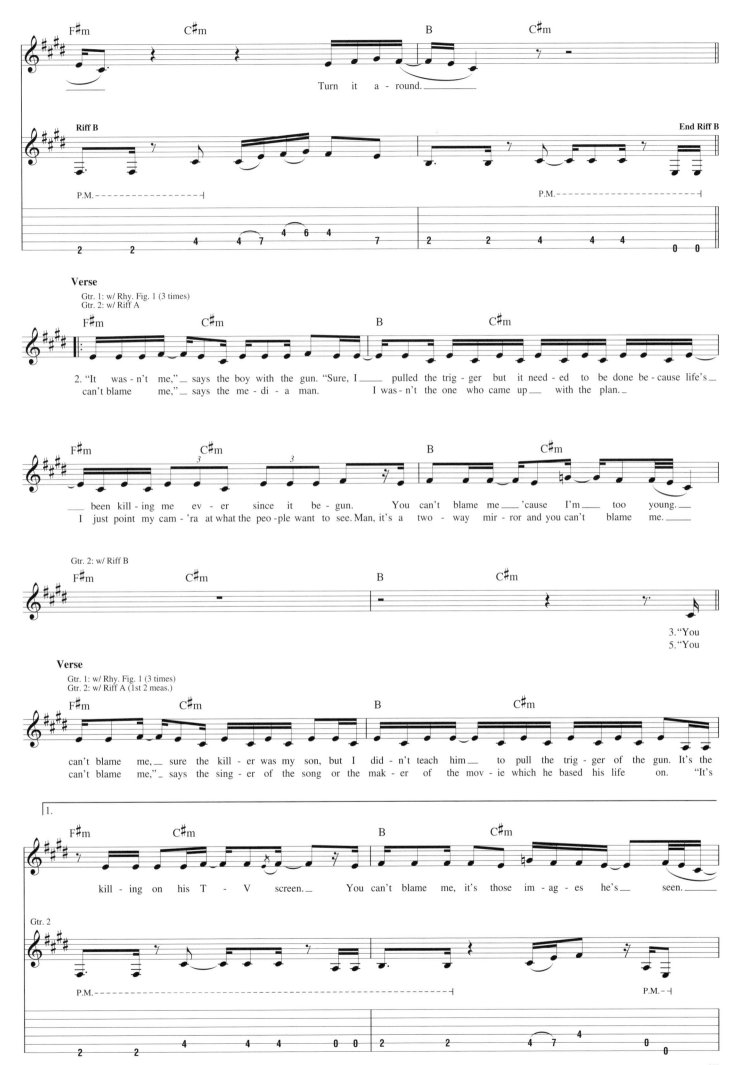

RODEO CLOWNS

Words and Music by
Jack Johnson

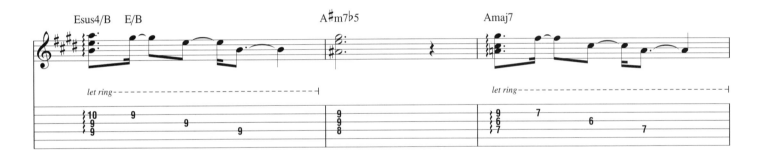

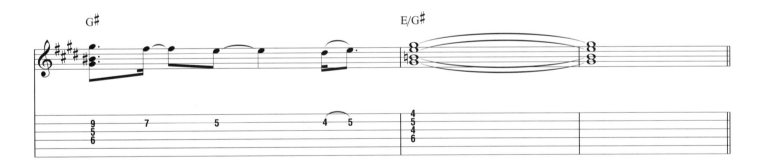

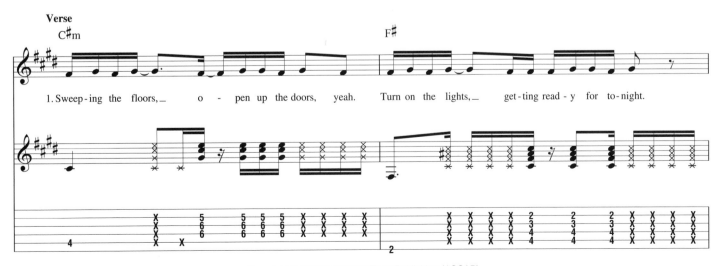

1. Sweep-ing the floors,__ o-pen up the doors, yeah. Turn on the lights,__ get-ting read-y for to-night.

Copyright © 2003 by Bubble Toes Publishing (ASCAP)
All Rights Administered by Universal Music Corp.
All Rights Reserved   Used by Permission

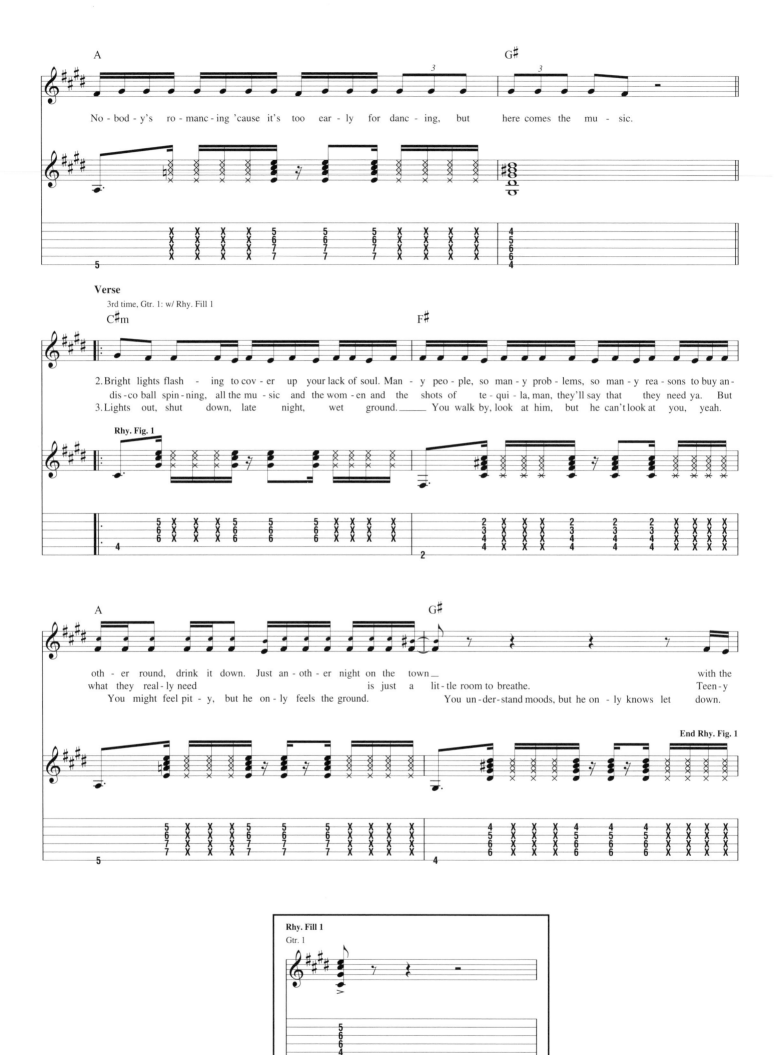

COCOON

Words and Music by
Jack Johnson

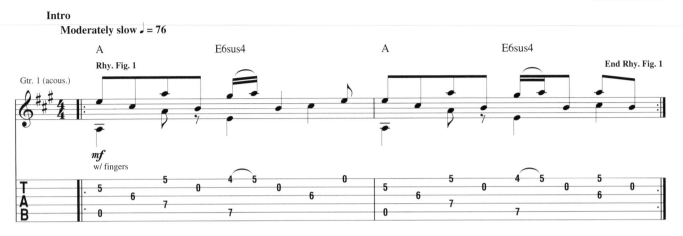

Copyright © 2003 by Bubble Toes Publishing (ASCAP)
All Rights Administered by Universal Music Corp.
All Rights Reserved   Used by Permission

Gtr. 1: w/ Rhy. Fig. 5

I guess it's all you knew, __ and all I had. __

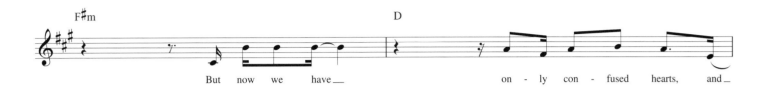

But now we have __ on - ly con - fused hearts, and __

D.S. al Coda

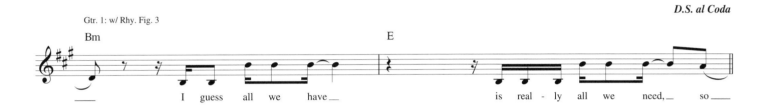

Gtr. 1: w/ Rhy. Fig. 3

__ I guess all we have __ is real - ly all we need, __ so __

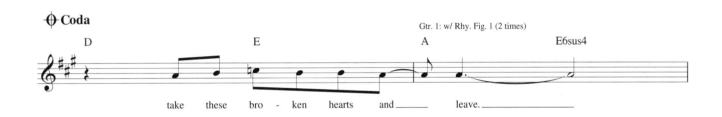

Coda

Gtr. 1: w/ Rhy. Fig. 1 (2 times)

take these bro - ken hearts and __ leave. __

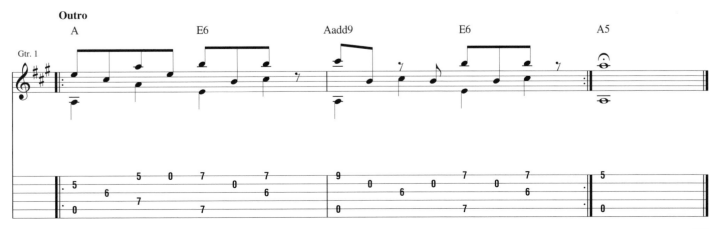

Outro

Gtr. 1

MEDIOCRE BAD GUYS

Words and Music by
Jack Johnson

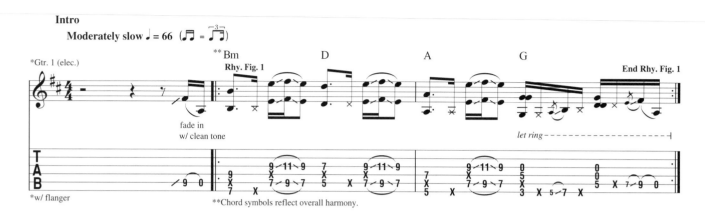

Copyright © 2003 by Bubble Toes Publishing (ASCAP)
All Rights Administered by Universal Music Corp.
All Rights Reserved   Used by Permission

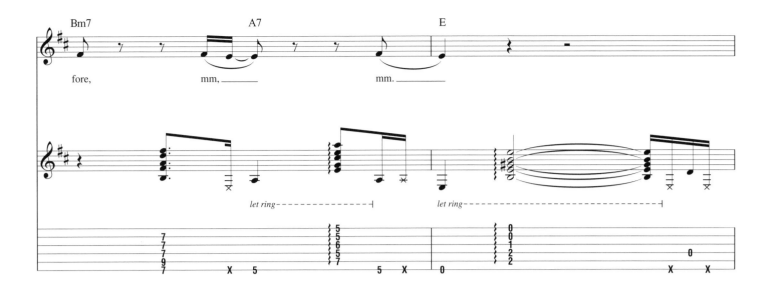

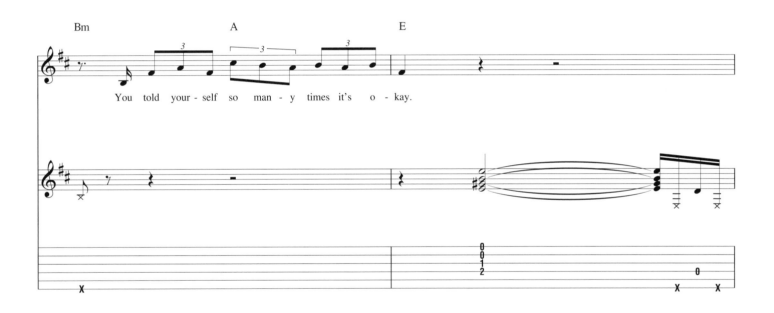

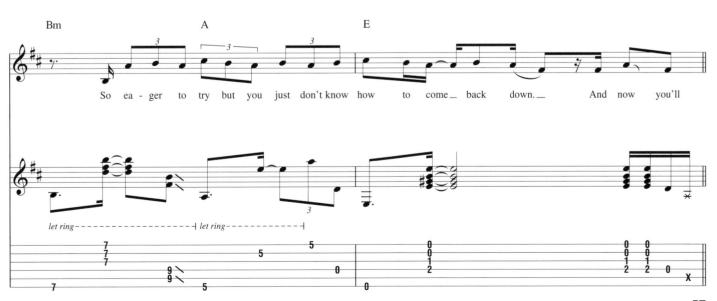

Chorus

beat me up and break me down, hop-ing I don't come a - round, kick me when I'm on the ground._

Beat me up and break me down, hop-ing I don't come a - round, kick me when I'm on the ground._
(Beat me up.   On the ground.)_

Guitar Solo

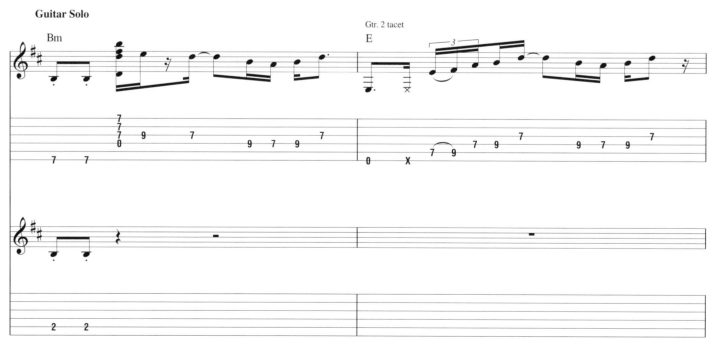

Verse

2. Well, how 'bout those peo - ple I know_ that you know_ the one's_ I mean:_ not so

good, not so bad, on - ly know what they have and they have on - ly what they've seen,_ aw.

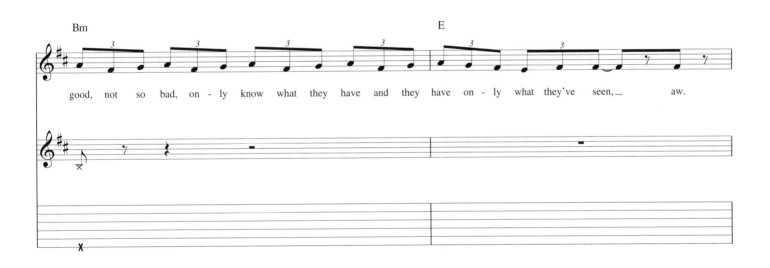

Them me - di - o - cre bad_ guys can real - ly_ bring you down._

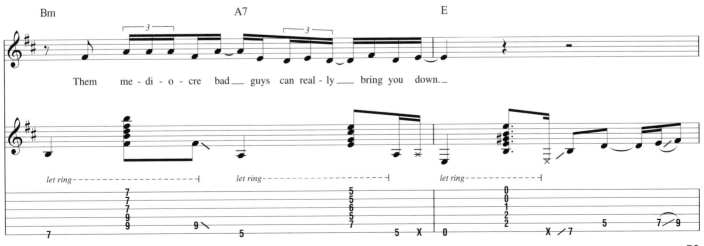

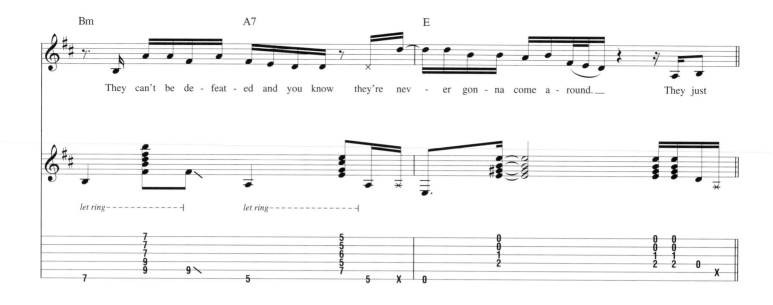

They can't be de-feat-ed and you know they're nev-er gon-na come a-round.___ They just

Chorus
Gtrs. 1 & 2: w/ Rhy. Figs. 2 & 2A

Beat me up and break me down, hop-ing I don't come a-round, kick me when I'm on the ground.___ They
(Beat me up.)

Gtrs. 1 & 2: w/ Rhy. Figs. 2 & 2A

*Voc. Fig. 1   End Voc. Fig. 1

beat me up and break me down, hop-ing I don't come a-round, kick me when I'm on the ground.___ They
(Beat me up,   break me down,   hop-ing I   don't come a-round.)___
*Refers to bkgd. voc. only.

Gtrs. 1 & 2: w/ Rhy. Figs. 2 & 2A (2 times)
Bkgd. Voc.: w/ Voc. Fig. 1 (2 times)
w/ Bkgd. Voc. ad lib

beat me up, break me down, hop-ing I don't come a-round, kick me when I'm on the ground. They

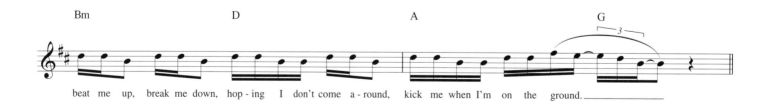

beat me up, break me down, hop-ing I don't come a-round, kick me when I'm on the ground.___

Outro
Gtrs. 1 & 2: w/ Rhy. Fig. 1

Repeat and fade

SYMBOL IN MY DRIVEWAY

Words and Music by
Jack Johnson

Copyright © 2003 by Bubble Toes Publishing (ASCAP)
All Rights Administered by Universal Music Corp.
All Rights Reserved   Used by Permission

62